ABOUT THIS BOOK

It is never too early to stress the importance of the environment and the need to care for every aspect of the natural world. Within the pages of this book you will find an exciting introduction to the wide variety of natural habitats found on our planet. Talk about each page with your child and discuss what is taking place. Point out the changes brought about by the weather and the seasons. Talk about the ways in which man can spoil the natural environment, and the things we can do to make the world a better place to live.

James Fitzsimmons
(Cert. Ed., Head of Infants)

Rhona Whiteford
(B.A. (Open), Cert. Ed., former Head of Infants)

the world of nature

written by
James Fitzsimmons and
Rhona Whiteford

illustrated by Terry Burton

Filmset in Nelson Teaching Alphabet
by kind permission of
Thomas Nelson and Son Ltd.

Published in Great Britain by World International Publishing Limited,
An Egmont Company, Egmont House, P.O. Box 111, Great Ducie Street,
Manchester M60 3BL.
Printed in DDR.
ISBN 0 7235 4119 1

A CIP catalogue record for this book is available from the British Library.

Spring in the garden

Spring is a busy time when birds make their nests and flowers begin to bloom.

Have you got a garden?

Summer on the seashore

Summer is the hot time of the year.
There are lots of exciting things to
look for on the seashore.

Do you like playing on the beach?

Autumn in the woods

In autumn the days become shorter,
the air is damp and leaves begin to
fall from the trees.

Do you think it would be fun to play in the autumn leaves?

Winter by the pond

Winter is a dark and cold time and it is hard for animals to find food.

Do you feed the birds in winter?

The desert

The desert is hot and dry.
The only place to find water is at
an oasis.
Many creatures live there.

Why do you think the children are
playing in the shade?

The mountain top

Mountain tops are very cold and the
highest ones are covered with snow
all the year round.

Green grass grows in the valley but only a few plants can grow on the rocky mountain top.

Under the sea

The bottom of the sea is an
exciting world.
It is like a colourful underwater
garden.

Many plants and creatures live side
by side.
How many different colours can
you see?

Under the ground

There are caves under the ground.
They are like big holes.
They are cold and dark and damp.

The rocks are strange and
wonderful shapes.
The creatures live in a world
of darkness.

The jungle

It is hot and steamy in the jungle and plants and flowers grow all year long.

Does your garden look like this?

Nature in the town

Plants grow in the strangest of places.

Soon this waste ground will be a garden of wild flowers.

Spoiling our world

Our beautiful world can be spoiled by
people who don't care.

Does your park look like this?

Caring for our world

Always put your litter in the bin.

You will help keep our world beautiful.

The world of nature never goes
to sleep, even at night.